WILLIAM

HOGARTH

MARRIAGE A LA MODE

And Other Engravings

Publishers *Lear* *New York*

MANUFACTURED IN THE UNITED STATES OF AMERICA

A NOTE ON HOGARTH

Foremost among those qualities which give Hogarth his position as the father of English social satire is his penetrating interest in contemporary life and his vigorous comment on it. Hogarth shares with the medieval engravers the popular manner of realistic story-telling combined with the fantastic but meaningful symbolism of the people. Hieronymus Bosch used these images to mirror the passions that stirred mankind on the eve of the Reformation. Half a century later, Peter Breughel drew on the same resources of fantasy and realism.

Hogarth's style, enriched by the vision of the great Flemish painters of the Sixteenth Century, fused the immemorial tradition of popular art with the latest innovations in painting. The Baroque artists of Hogarth's day were superb illusionists. By clever disposition of light and space, the Baroque decorators led the spectator's eye away from the solid bricks of the street into the billowing clouds where angels and saints hover around the scene of some latter day miracle. The intention of Baroque art was to make us forget the material scene and ascend into a spiritual realm conjured up by every trick of pictorial stagecraft.

But Hogarth's actors are not creatures of the clouds. They are the artisans and tradesmen, the soldiers and politicians, the beggars, the thieves and the idle rich of Eighteenth Century London. To set off his teeming scenes so rich in interplay of earthy plots and conflicts, Hogarth created a compact, box-like stage which could be viewed frontally. Whatever Hogarth employs from the Baroque bag of tricks he puts to work to enclose his space within the solid walls of London's streets. Witness the design with which the eye is carried, step by step, past alternating structures, from each side of the street to the towering steeple in the background of *Gin Lane*. Uncompromising realism is the trademark of the Hogarth tradition.

What gives these engravings their character of earth-bound reality is quickly seen in the great cycle of *The Rake's* and *Harlot's Progress*, in *Marriage a la Mode* and in the story of the *Idle* and *Industrious Apprentices* (1732-1747). Hogarth depicts the society of his period on three distinct levels; high life, low life and what has been called by Defoe, "the middle station." In Hogarth's scale of values both extremes meet. In both, men seek in vain to live in luxury without work. In both idleness leads to disaster. Such is the fate of the Harlot, the Idle Apprentice and the dissolute nobleman. Industry is rewarded in the attainment of the "middle station" which is blessed by "all agreeable diversions and all desirable pleasures."

Hogarth was evidently advocating the values and vitality of the craftsmen, the farmers, merchants and conscientious squires, whose singleminded energy compelled the Industrial Revolution that transformed the face of English Society. "He that does not work, neither shall he eat." This is the essential morality of the "middle station." Hogarth underlines this time-honored adage with a wealth of observation. His engravings are peopled with representatives of the extremes in society, yet he does not neglect the vices of his own "middle station." In the contrast of mass distress and individual advancement which accompanied England's expanding textile idustry, even Goodchild, the Industrious Apprentice, must clinch his career by marrying the master's daughter.

Hogarth shows the circumstances of life, not by formula, but as they actually were, infinitely varied as the characters of living men.

THE PUBLISHERS

The authentic and colorful commentaries accompanying the engravings are from one of the earliest printed editions of Hogarth's complete works. Their intention is to round out the story and folkways which each of the cycles and individual engravings reveals. These didactic sermons are an ingenuous reflection of the morality of England's rising middle class at the turn of the Nineteenth Century.

THE MARRIAGE-A-LA-MODE.

PLATE I.

ALTHOUGH there is no act in our life of greater importance to us, nor one on which our happiness depends, more than that of marriage; yet so rash and presumptive are we, that we pay little regard to it, otherwise than as it suits or clashes with our interest. In order, however, to create in us an abhorrence of lucrative alliances, when formed under that consideration only, and to shew the folly of seeking matrimonial connections chiefly with pecuniary views, Mr. Hogarth has in the following scenes exhibited, in the most striking colours, the fatal end of what he calls a Marriage-a-la-mode; which being so general and fashionable a thing among us, the term is too appropriate to savour of the least impropriety: and because this folly is more conspicuous among the great, he has taken his subject from high life, and has drawn it with the pencil of truth.

We are then to suppose that an immensely rich Alderman of the City of London, whose wealth was acquired by trade, had for some time, in order to ennoble his family, been desirous of a matrimonial alliance with the family of some man of fashion, who with a view of recruiting his wasted fortune, might readily accept his proposals. We may easily imagine that it was not long before he met with the wished-for opportunity, there being many of the English nobility with encumbered estates, always prepared to embrace such an offer. View then the wealthy Cit, all necessary preliminaries being adjusted, at the house of a British Earl, signing and sealing the marriage settlement, and paying his daughter's stipulated fortune. See him with all the appearance of a person of property, accustomed to the tale of money, casting his eye on what his clerk, an old faithful servant, has just counted down. On the other hand behold the Peer, the father of the bridegroom, full of his titles and nobility.

Hogarth pinx!   T. Cook sculp!

MARRIAGE A LA MODE.

PLATE II.

THAT indifference which precedes a marriage of this sort, seldom fails to follow it. When we unite ourselves by contract, we would generally live separate by inclination. Tired of one another, nothing is more common than for the husband to grow sick of home, to stay out until a late hour in the evening, and for the wife to wear away the tedious hours by entertainments, cards, and other acts of dissipation.

This plate then, before us, represents a saloon in this young nobleman's house, not long after the breaking up of one of these card parties. The clock shews us it is noon. We are to suppose then by the candles being still burning, that the day had been shut out, and converted into night; a circumstance not a little characteristic of the irregularity and disorder that reign within the house; and that after an hour or two's sleep, madam is just risen to breakfast; whose rising has occasioned that of the family in general. This is intimated by one of the servants in the back ground of this plate, who we are to understand, though scarce awake, has hurried on his cloaths, in order to set the house in some measure to rights. By the treatise of Hoyle upon the floor, we are taught the idle study of people of distinction, to whom books in general are disgusting, unless they tend to dissipation, or serve to instruct them in their favourite amusements. With respect to the attitudes of the two principal figures, the fineness of the thought, and the particular exactness of the expressions, they must be allowed to be extremely beautiful. They are at the same time well introduced, as from the indifference that gives rise to them, springs the destruction of this unhappy family. On the one hand we are to suppose the lady actuated by soft desire, totally neglected by her husband; on the other, by way of contrast, that the husband is just returned from the apartments of some woman, fatigued, exhausted, and satiated. And as pleasures of this sort are seldom without interruption, we are shewn by the female cap in his pocket, and his broken sword, that he has been engaged in some riot or uproar.

Hogarth pinx.ᵗ   T. Cook & Son. sc.

MARRIAGE A LA MODE.

PLATE III.

DISEASE is universally the attendant of debauchery. Our author has therefore introduced us to the hero of this piece, at the house of an empiric, where he would have had no occasion to be, had it not been for his lewd course of life. He has brought with him two females, with whom he has been acquainted, that the doctor might determine to which of the two he might attribute his disorder. His being prejudiced in favour of the girl, occasions a quarrel between him and the woman, which proceeds to great height, even to that of blows. The doctor, unconcerned at this dispute, and solicitous for little but himself, increases the noise, by thundering to the mute-struck girl, " Vat?—you won't take your *pe—els ?*" angry to think his medicines are so little regarded. The contrast between this girl and the woman is exceedingly beautiful: the age, the timidity, the softness of the one; the rage, the fury, and the harshness of the other, are strongly characteristic of the simplicity that dwells in those who are strangers to vice, and the natural ferocity inherent in such as are long habituated to it. Though both the quack and his apartments are objects rather foreign to the purpose, yet Mr. Hogarth has taken this opportunity of ridiculing the folly of such men, as enter upon a profession with which they are wholly unacquainted; and, by representing this empiric, as a Frenchman, censures the government of this kingdom, for tolerating a foreigner to exercise an art here which he would not be permitted to do in his own country. Although he was formerly a barber, he is now, if we may judge by the appearance of his his house, not only a surgeon, but a naturalist, chemist, mechanic, physician, and apothecary; and, to complete the character, he is supposed to have invented two machines, extremely complicate, for the most simple operations; one to set a dislocated limb, the other, to uncork a bottle. On the first of the two lies a folio treatise on the nature of these instruments, in French, whose title page is, " An Explanation of the Two Grand Machines, one for Re-setting the Collar-Bone, the other for Drawing a Cork: invented by Monsieur *De la Pillule:* inspected and approved by the Royal Academy at Paris."

MARRIAGE A LA MODE.

Hogarth pinx.^t

T. Cook sculp.^t

PLATE IV.

THE old nobleman is now supposed to be dead, and the young Lord in the entire possession of his estate. In consequence of this, he launches out into every species of fashionable extravagance and folly, has his levees, his routs, &c. and is entirely a dupe to the foibles of his dissipated wife.

See, then, in this fourth plate, a groupe of figures highly amusing. We shall begin with the principal, that of madam, at her toilette, under the hands of her French valet-de-chambre. By the china figures on the floor, which her black boy has brought home, she is supposed to be just returned from one of those auctions or sales of old goods, at which places women of quality are generally duped. 'Tis pride only, and a determination of rivalling their acquaintance in expence that cause them to buy, or they would not purchase, as they often do, at an exorbitant price, an antique jar, or an ugly pagod, which they have not the least occasion for, and which have neither beauty nor value to recommend them. Let any one cast an eye on the various lots, and observe the precious acquisition our heroine has made, which, by the catalogue on the floor, seems to have been once the property of Sir *Timothy Baby-house*, and we are persuaded he must think the same. Among these is a porcelaine figure of Actæon, to whose horns the boy, with a leer upon his lady, is archly pointing, as emblematical of of the ridiculous appearance of his master. It has ever been foolishly considered, among the first rank of people, as a mark of grandeur, to have frequently, at their houses, one of those melodious animals, which are brought from Italy at a vast expence: there is such a one here singing, and is particularly well delineated for one of those unfortunate wretches, that too often fall a victim to the musical madness of the Italians. His diamond buckles, rings, solitaire, and ear-rings, tell us the many valuable presents the ladies have made him, who are generally fond of any thing they think uncommon. As a proof of this, see Lady Charlotte almost fainting with the ravishing sound of this melodious singer, and the mellow notes of the warbling flute. Not so the country gentleman on her left, who, having no relish for these exalted pleasures, is fallen fast asleep.

Hogarth pinxt   T. Cook & Son sc.

MARRIAGE A LA MODE.

PLATE V.

THE fatal consequence of going to the masquerade, is here shewn to perfection. The ticket was accepted to favour an assignation; the assignation took place, and the catastrophe is dire. Happy was our heroine to find an opportunity of enjoying the company of her spark; happy was the barrister to take an advantage of the supposed weakness of her husband; but behold the end of such illicit and unwarrantable proceedings!—They are supposed to have retired from the ball to some bagnio, in order to gratify their illicit amours. But what are we to imagine brought the husband here?—Suspicion, and an eagerness to know the truth. Her indiscreet behaviour had long given birth to jealousy, and her going to this place of amusement without him confirmed it. Determined to see the extent of her misconduct, he secretly follows her from his house to the masquerade, from the masquerade to the bagnio; rashly gives them an opportunity of undressing, that he might have the satisfaction of discovering them in bed. Had he shewn himself at their entrance into the house, it might have answered his purpose equally well, and, in all probability, this scene would have been prevented; but, instead of this, he goes after them to the chamber, and thirsting for revenge, unsheaths his sword, bursts open the door, and attacks his rival, who was also prepared in case of any interruption; a thrust or two passes between them, and the husband is wounded mortally. The noise this occasioned brings up the watch and a servant of the house, who seem thunderstruck at the ghastly spectacle: alarmed at this accident, the young counsellor secures himself, by escaping from the window in his shirt; and his mistress, struck by remorse and horror, falls on her knees to her dying husband, and wringing her hands, with tears in her eyes, and with fluttering accents, confesses her guilt, imploring his forgiveness. Now, though too late, begins to work that sorrow, which, had it found its way to her breast before, might have prevented this dreadful act, and, perhaps, been the basis of their future happiness; but, on the contrary, she pursued her vicious inclinations, even to the death of her husband.

MARRIAGE A LA MODE.

PLATE VI.

THOUGH the young barrister fled from the window, it was of no avail; he reaches the ground 'tis true, but is presently taken by the watch, and the next day committed to prison, there to bewail his past imprudence, and settle his accounts with his Creator. Madam is conducted to her house, and left to repent her past folly and wickedness. On the report of this melancholy story, the tradesmen of her Lord (who had long foreborn carrying matters to extremities) become urgent and clamorous in their demands. She, therefore, not being disposed to settle their accounts in this situation, makes a friend of her father, throws her affairs into his hands, leaves her home, and returns to his house, supposed to be somewhere near London-bridge, for we have a view of it from the window in its original state, when covered with houses. We shall pass over the many sad hours she is presumed to wear away in hateful meditation, and hasten to the scene before us, a scene of aggravated distress and horror. Left to the dreaded leisure of her thoughts, she becomes conscious of having been the destruction of her husband, of her lover, (for by the dying speech before her, we are told he has been tried and executed) her reputation, and her happiness; and foolishly thinks she has no other refuge from the terrors of her mind than to destroy *herself*. Unhappy situation, to have least reason and resolution when we stand in need of them! Little does she reflect upon the consequences of so presumptive an act, but hopes only to ease the anguish of her mind, by depriving herself of the power of thinking. In this disordered state she artfully sends a servant for a dose of laudanum, swallows it, and puts an end to her now miserable existence. Behold her then, in the last moments of her life, seized with death, as she and her father were sitting down to dinner. A physician and apothecary are immediately sent for, but all their assistance is vain, it being now too late.

Hogarth pinx.t   T. Cook & Son sc.

MARRIAGE A LA MODE.

PLATE I.

THE FELLOW-'PRENTICES AT THEIR LOOMS.

"The drunkard shall come to poverty, and drowsiness shall clothe a man with rags."   *Proverbs, Chap.* xxiii. *Verse* 21.
" The hand of the diligent maketh rich."   *Proverbs, Chap.* x. *Verse* 4.

———

THE first print presents us with a noble and striking contrast in two apprentices at the looms of their master, a silk weaver of Spitalfields: in the one we observe a serene and open countenance, the distinguishing mark of innocence; and in the other a sullen, down-cast look, the index of a corrupt mind and vicious heart. The industrious youth is diligently employed at his work, and his thoughts taken up with the business he is upon. His book, called, the *'Prentice's Guide,* supposed to be given him for instruction, lies open beside him, as if perused with care and attention. The employment of the day seems his constant study; and the interest of his master his continual regard. We are given to understand, also, by the ballads, of the *London* 'Prentice, *Whittington* the Mayor, &c. that hang behind him, that he lays out his pence on things that may improve his mind, and enlighten his understanding. On the contrary, his fellow-'prentice, with worn-out coat and uncombed hair, overpowered with beer, indicated by the half-gallon pot before him, is fallen asleep; and from the shuttle becoming the plaything of the wanton kitten, we learn how he slumbers on, inattentive alike to his own and his master's interest. The ballad of *Moll Flanders,* on the wall behind him, shews that the bent of his mind is towards that which is bad; and his book of instructions lying torn and defaced upon the ground, manifests how regardless he is of any thing tending to his future welfare. His master's entering the room with angry countenance, and uplifted cane, shews that his indolence and sloth are visited with present chastisement; while a pair of fetters, a cat-o'-nine-tails and a halter, are emblematical of what he may expect in future; whereas on the other side, the golden chain, the sword and mace, are introduced to shew that preferment and honour are the rewards of diligence and industry.

INDUSTRY AND IDLENESS.

PLATE V.

THE IDLE 'PRENTICE TURNED AWAY AND SENT TO SEA

" A foolish son is the heaviness of his mother."   *Proverbs, Chap.* x. *Verse* 1.

CORRUPTED by sloth and contaminated by evil company, the idle apprentice, having tired the patience of his master, is sent to sea, in the hope that the being removed from the vices of the town, and the influence of his wicked companions, joined with the hardships and perils of a sea-faring life, might effect that reformation of which his friends despaired while he continued on shore. See him then in the ship's boat, accompanied by his afflicted mother, making towards the vessel in which he is to embark. The disposition of the different figures in the boat, and the expression of their countenances, tell us plainly, that his evil pursuits and incorrigible wickedness are the subjects of their discourse. The waterman significantly directs his attention to a figure on a gibbet, as emblematical of his future fate, should he not turn from the evil of his ways ; and the boy shews him a cat-o'-nine-tails, expressive of the discipline that awaits him on board of ship; these admonitions, however, he notices only by the application of his fingers to his forehead, in the form of horns, jestingly telling them to look at *Cuckold's Point*, which they have just past ; he then throws his indentures into the water with an air of contempt, that proves how little he is affected by his present condition, and how little he regards the persuasions and tears of a fond mother, whose heart seems ready to burst with grief at the fate of her darling son, and perhaps her only stay ; for her dress seems to intimate that she is a widow Well then might Solomon say, that, " *a foolish son is the heaviness of his mother ;*" for we here behold her who had often rejoiced in the prospect of her child being a prop to her in the decline of life, lamenting his depravity, and anticipating with horror the termination of his evil course.

Hogarth pinx.

T. Cook sculp.

INDUSTRY AND IDLENESS.

PLATE VI.

THE INDUSTRIOUS 'PRENTICE OUT OF HIS TIME, AND MARRIED TO HIS MASTER'S DAUGHTER.

"The virtuous woman is a crown to her husband."   *Proverbs, Chap.* xii. *Verse* 4.

———

WE now return with pleasure to the industrious youth, increasing in happiness, and as a reward for his diligence, taken into partnership by his master (evident from the joint names upon the sign) and married to his daughter; the subject of this plate being finely continued from the second and fourth. By the young man's appearing in his cap and gown at break-fast, in company with his amiable spouse, we are to suppose it morning; and by the congratulations of the mob, (gathered in great numbers, by the report of his benevolence and generosity,) the morning after marriage. Even in this hour of hilarity, in this feast and riot of the senses, he is not inattentive to the distresses of others, nor deaf to the voice of humanity. The natural feelings of his heart, and his desire that others should in some measure partake of his felicity, are visible from the servant's distributing by his desire to the necessitous, and giving to the master drummer gold to gladden the hearts of his comrades. In this group of figures the true spirit of this nation is exquisitely described, in the earnestness with which one of the butchers, standing with his marrow-bone and cleaver, observes the fortunate receiver for the drums; and in the anger expressed in the countenance of his fellow, who is elbowing out of the first rank the ruffled French performer on the base-viol, demanding that precedence the English have always enjoyed. The cripple on the left of this was intended for a well-known beggar, called *Philip-in-the-tub*, (from his being reduced to this shift we see in order to supply his unhappy loss of limbs) who in the principal towns of Ireland and the Seven-Provinces, as well as those in Great Britain, was a constant attendant at all weddings, as an epithalamist. He is supposed to be here bawling out the old song of *Jesse, or the Happy Pair*.

INDUSTRY AND IDLENESS.

PLATE VII.

THE IDLE 'PRENTICE RETURNED FROM SEA, AND IN A GARRET WITH A COMMON PROSTITUTE.

" The sound of a shaken leaf shall chase him."   *Leviticus, Chap.* xxvi. *Verse* 6.

———

THE idle apprentice, as appears by this print, is advancing with rapid strides towards his fate. We are to suppose him returned from sea after a long voyage; and to have met with such correction abroad for his obstinacy, during his absence from England, that though it was found insufficient to alter his disposition, yet it determined him to pursue some other way of life; and what he entered on is here but too evident (from the pistols by the bed-side, and the trinkets his companion is examining, in order to strip him of) to be that of the highway. He is represented in a garret, with a common prostitute, the partaker of his infamy, awaking, after a night spent in robbery and plunder, from one of those broken slumbers which are ever the consequences of a life of dishonesty and debauchery. Though the designs of providence are visible in every thing, yet they are never more conspicuous than in this; that whatever these unhappy wretches possess by wicked and illegal means, they seldom comfortably enjoy. In this scene we have one of the finest pictures imaginable of the horrors of a guilty conscience. Though the door is fastened in the strongest manner with a lock and two bolts, and with the addition of some planks from the flooring, so as to make his retreat as secure as possible; though he has attempted to drive away thought by the powerful effects of spirituous liquors, plain from the glass and bottle upon the floor, still he is not able to brave out his guilt, or steel his breast against reflection. Behold him roused by the accidental circumstance of a cat's coming down the chimney, and the falling of a few bricks, which he believes to be the noise of his pursuers! Observe his starting up in bed, and all the tortures of his mind imprinted in his face!

INDUSTRY AND IDLENESS.

PLATE IX.

THE IDLE 'PRENTICE BETRAYED BY A PROSTITUTE, AND TAKEN IN A NIGHT CELLAR WITH HIS ACCOMPLICE.

"The adultress will hunt for precious life."   *Proverbs, Chap.* vi. *Verse* 26.

———

FROM the picture of the reward of Diligence, we return to take a further view of the progress of Sloth and Infamy; by following the idle 'prentice a step nearer to the approach of his unhappy end. We see him in the third plate herding with the worst of the human species, the very dregs of the people; one of his companions, at that time, being a one-eyed wretch, who seemed hackneyed in the ways of vice. To break this vile connection he was sent to sea; but, no sooner did he return, than his wicked disposition took its natural course, and every day he lived served only to habituate him to acts of greater criminality. He presently discovered his old acquaintance, who, no doubt, rejoiced to find him so ripe for mischief: with this worthless abandoned fellow, he enters into engagements of the worst kind, even those of robbery and murder. Thus blindly will men sometimes run headlong to their own destruction!

About the time when these plates were first published, which was in the year 1747, there was a noted house in Chick Lane, Smithfield, that went by the name of the *Blood-Bowl House*, so called from the numerous scenes of blood that were almost daily carried on there; it being a receptacle for prostitutes and thieves; where every species of delinquency was practised; and where, indeed, there seldom passed a month without the commission of some act of murder. To this subterraneous abode of iniquity (it being a cellar) was our hero soon introduced; where he is now represented in company with his accomplice, and others of the same stamp, having just committed a most horrid act of barbarity, (that of killing a passer-by, and conveying him into a place under ground, contrived for this purpose,) dividing among them the ill-gotten booty.

INDUSTRY AND IDLENESS.

PLATE X.

THE INDUSTRIOUS 'PRENTICE ALDERMAN OF LONDON; THE IDLE ONE BROUGHT BEFORE HIM, AND IMPEACHED BY HIS ACCOMPLICE.

"Thou shalt do no unrighteousness in judgment."   *Leviticus, Chap.* xix. *Verse* 15.
"The wicked is snared in the work of his own hands."   *Psalms, Chap.* ix. *Verse* 16.

IMAGINE now this depraved and atrocious youth hand-cuffed, and dragged from his wicked haunt, through the streets to a place of security, amidst the scorn and contempt of a jeering populace; and thence brought before the sitting magistrate, (who, to heighten the scene and support the contrast, is supposed to be his fellow-'prentice, now chosen an alderman) in order to be dealt with according to law. See him then at last, having run his course of iniquity, fallen into the hands of justice, being betrayed by his accomplice; a further proof of the perfidy of man, when even partners in vice are unfaithful to each other. This is the only print among the set, excepting the first, where the two principal characters are introduced; in which Mr. Hogarth has shewn his great abilities, as well in description, as in a particular attention to the uniformity and connection of the whole. He is now at the bar, with all the marks of guilt imprinted on his face. How, if his fear will permit him to reflect, must he think on the happiness and exaltation of his fellow-'prentice on the one hand, and of his own misery and degradation on the other; at one instant, he condemns the persuasions of his wicked companions; at another, his own idleness and obstinacy: however, deeply smitten with his crime, he sues the magistrate, upon his knees, for mercy, and pleads in his cause the former acquaintance that subsisted between them, when they both dwelt beneath the same roof, and served the same common master: but here was no room for lenity, murder was his crime, and death must be his punishment; the proofs are incontestible, and his *mittimus* is ordered, which the clerk is drawing out.

Hogarth pinx!

INDUSTRY AND IDLENESS.

PLATE XI.

THE IDLE 'PRENTICE EXECUTED AT TYBURN.

" When fear cometh as desolation, and their destruction cometh as a whirlwind : when distress cometh upon them,
" then shall they call upon God, but he will not answer."   *Proverbs, Chap.* i. *Verse* 7 and 8.

———

THUS after a life of sloth, wretchedness and vice, does our delinquent terminate his career.   Behold him, on the dreadful morn of execution, drawn in a cart (attended by the sheriff's officers on horseback, with his coffin behind him,) through the public streets to Tyburn, there to receive the just reward of his crimes, a shameful ignominious death.   The ghastly appearance of his face, and the horror painted on his countenance, plainly shew the dreadful situation of his mind ; which, we must imagine, to be agitated with shame, remorse, confusion and terror.   The careless position of the Ordinary at the coach window, is intended to show how inattentive those appointed to that office are of their duty, giving room for heresy, which is excellently expressed by the itinerant preacher in the cart, instructing from a book of Wesley's.   Mr. Hogarth has in this print, digressing from the history and moral of the piece, taken an opportunity of giving us a humorous representation of an execution, or a Tyburn Fair ; such days being made holidays, produce scenes of the greatest riot, disorder and uproar ; being generally attended by hardened wretches who go there, not so much to reflect upon their own vices, as to commit those crimes which must in time inevitably bring them to the same shameful end.   In confirmation of this, see how earnestly one boy watches the motions of the man selling his cakes, while he is picking his pocket ; and another waiting to receive the booty! We have here interspersed before us a deal of low humour, but such as is common on occasions like this.   In one place we observe an old bawd turning up her eyes and drinking a glass of gin, the very picture of hypocrisy ; and a man indecently helping up a girl into the same cart : in another, a soldier sunk up to his knees in a bog, and two boys laughing at him, are well imagined.

INDUSTRY & IDLENESS.

PLATE XII.

THE INDUSTRIOUS 'PRENTICE LORD MAYOR OF LONDON.

" Length of days is in her right hand, and in her left hand riches and honour."   *Proverbs, Chap.* iii. *Verse* 16.

HAVING seen the ignominious end of the idle apprentice, nothing remains but to represent the completion of the other's happiness; who is now exalted to the highest honour, that of Lord Mayor of London; the greatest reward that ancient and noble city can bestow on diligence and integrity.   Our artist has here, as in the last plate, given a loose to his humour, in representing more of the low part of the Lord Mayor's show, than the magnificent; yet the honour done the city, by the presence of the Prince and Princess of Wales is not forgot.   The variety of comic characters in this print, serves to shew what generally passes on such public processions as these, when the people collect to gratify their childish curiosity and indulge their wanton disposition, or natural love of riot. The front of this plate exhibits the oversetting of a board, on which some girls had stood, and represents them sprawling upon the ground; on the left, at the back of the scaffold, is a fellow saluting a fair nymph, and another enjoying the joke : near him is a blind man straggled in among the crowd, and joining in the general hollow : before him is a militia-man, so completely intoxicated as not to know what he is doing ; a figure of infinite humour.   Though Mr. Hogarth has here marked out two or three particular things, yet his chief intention was to ridicule the city militia, which was at this period composed of undisciplined men, of all ages, sizes, and height ; some fat, some lean, some tall, some short, some crooked, some lame, and in general so unused to muskets that they knew not how to carry them.   One, we observe, is firing his piece and turning his head another way, at whom the man above is laughing, and at which the child is frightened.   The boy on the right, crying, " a full and true account of the ghost of Thomas Idle," which is supposed to have appeared to the Mayor, preserves the connection of the whole work.

Hogarth pinx.ᵗ   T. Cook sculp

INDUSTRY & IDLENESS.

THE FOUR STAGES OF CRUELTY.

PLATE 1.

FIRST STAGE OF CRUELTY.

" While various scenes of sportive woe
  " The infant race employ;
" And tortur'd victims bleeding shew
  " The *tyrant* in the boy.

" Behold a youth of gentler heart,
  " To spare the creature's pain,
" O take, he cries—take all my tart,
  " But tears and tart are vain.

" Learn from this fair example, you
  " Who savage sports delight,
" How CRUELTY disgusts the view,
  " While PITY charms the sight."

THOUGH humanity is the distinguishing characteristic of the British nation; (we mean that part of it which we call the better sort of people,) yet the lower class of Britons are not less remarkable for their studied barbarity, insomuch that foreigners have frequently taken notice of the cruelty of English pastimes, which we certainly must have derived from the Goths and Scythians: but one would imagine as the times grew more civilized, this merciless disposition would have gradually decreased; whereas, on the contrary, we grow more sanguinary, and indulge our savage inclinations at the expence of all that is rational, humane, and religious. Does not the epicure even torture the creature to pamper his voluptuous palate? Are not lobsters roasted alive, pigs whipped to death, and fowls sewed up!

FIRST STAGE OF CRUELTY.

PLATE II.

SECOND STAGE OF CRUELTY.

———

" The generous steed in hoary age,
  " Subdued by labour lies,
" And mourns a cruel master's rage,
  " While nature strength denies.

" The tender lamb, o'er-drove and faint,
  " Amidst expiring throes,
" Bleats forth its innocent complaint,
  " And dies beneath the blows.

" Inhuman wretch! Say, whence proceeds
  " This coward cruelty?
" What interest springs from barbarous deeds?
  " What joy from misery!"

THE spirit of inhumanity which we observed in the preceding plate growing up in youth, is in this ripened by manhood; here we see Tom Nero, the hero of our piece, become a hackney-coachman, a profession in which he has an opportunity of displaying his brutal disposition. He is here shewn cruelly beating one of his poor horses for not rising; though in its fall, by over-setting the coach, it has had the misfortune to break its leg; and so sensible is the afflicted creature of the unkindness of his master, that we perceive the big round drop trickling down his cheek, a manifest proof of his inward feelings. Pity is it that such barbarous wretches should be suffered to live! However, his behaviour attracts the notice of a passer-by, who is taking the number of his coach, in order to have him punished. The humane countenance of this man, opposed to the rigid severe one of the other, affords us an agreeable contrast, and keeps up the spirit of the piece.

THE SECOND STAGE OF CRUELTY.

PLATE III.

CRUELTY IN PERFECTION.

———

" To lawless love, when once betray'd,
  " Soon crime to crime succeeds;
" At length beguil'd to theft, the maid
  " By her *beguiler* bleeds.

" Yet learn, seducing men, not night,
  " With all its sable cloud,
" Can skreen the guilty deeds from sight,
  " Foul murder cries aloud!

" The gaping wounds, the blood-stain'd steel,
  " Now shock his trembling soul,
" But ah! what pangs his breast must feel
  " When death his knell shall toll!"

CONTINUED acts of barbarity are found in time to divest men of their natural feelings; for he that would not hesitate to torture and destroy a harmless, helpless animal, would not, but through fear of the law, scruple to murder a fellow-creature. Nay, the laws themselves are not able to prevent such horrid crimes. As a proof of this, Mr. Hogarth describes the hero of this piece arrived at such a state of vice, as to be past feeling; no tenderness is supposed to affect him, no sense of distress to move him. Let us then take a view of cruelty in perfection, and see to what horrid lengths his disposition has carried him. As a hackney-coachman, his barbarity did not pass unnoticed; his treatment of his horses became publicly known, and was attended with a discharge from his place: being therefore at a loss for a maintenance, his wicked turn of mind soon led him upon the road, which is shewn by the pistols and watches found upon him. During the time he followed this iniquitous career, we are to suppose him to have made himself acquainted with a young woman, a servant to some lady residing in the country, whom we are to imagine he deceived by lies and false protestations.

Hogarth pinxt   T Cook sculpt

CRUELTY IN PERFECTION.

PLATE IV.

THE REWARD OF CRUELTY.

———————

" Behold the villain's dire disgrace,
  " Not death itself can end,
" He finds no peaceful burial-place,
  " His breathless corse—no friend.

" Torn from the root, that wicked *tongue*,
  " Which daily swore and curst;
" Those eye-balls from their sockets wrung,
  " That glow'd with lawless lust.

" His heart exposed to prying eyes,
  " To pity has no claim;
" But, dreadful! from his bones shall rise
  " His monument of shame."

HAVING shewn the progress of cruelty in different stages, our author comes now to the punishment that awaits its perpetrator. He is condemned to die by the laws of his country, and is conveyed to the place of execution; afterwards sent to Surgeon's Hall for dissection. He is now under the Surgeon's hands, and a lecture being read upon his body. Behold, and shudder at the ghastly sight! See his tongue pulled from the root, his eye-balls wrung from their sockets, and his heart torn from his body, which the dog is gnawing beneath the table! To give us a true idea of this scene of horror, in one place a man is pulling the entrails into a bucket, in another, some sculls and bones are boiling in a caldron, by way of cleaning and whitening them, in order to have them linked together by wires, as they were connected in the human frame. Two of these skeletons we observe above, whom our author has humourously described as pointing, with a grin to the Physician's or Surgeon's Arms upon the chair; *viz.* a hand feeling the pulse, intimating that death is too often the consequence of our too great opinion of these self-important nature menders.

Hogarth pinx.   T. Cook sculp.

THE REWARD OF CRUELTY.

THE RAKE'S PROGRESS.

PLATE I.

" Oh, vanity of age untoward!
" Ever spleeny, ever froward!
" Why these bolts and massy chains,
" Squint suspicions, jealous pains?
" Why, thy toilsome journey o'er,
" Lay'st thou up an useless store?
" *Hope*, along with *Time* is flown;
" Nor canst thou reap the field thou'st sown.
" Hast thou a son? In time be wise;
" He views thy toil with other eyes.
" Needs must thy kind paternal care,
" Lock'd in thy chests, be buried there?
" Whence, then, shall flow that friendly ease,
" That social converse, heartfelt peace,
" Familiar duty without dread,
" Instruction from example bred,
" Which youthful minds with freedom mend,
" And with the *father* mix the *friend*.
" Uncircumscrib'd by prudent rules,
" Or precepts of expensive schools;
" Abus'd at home, abroad despis'd,
" Unbred, unletter'd, unadvis'd;
" The headstrong course of life begun,
" What comfort from thy darling son?"

HOADLEY

IN the preceding series of prints we have had an able delineation of the progressive rewards of virtue, and sure punishment of vice. In the present series our author has traced the certain consequences of prodigality. In the first plate we have an excellent representation of a young heir taking possession of a miser's effects. The scene crowded with all the monuments of avarice, exhibits a thoughtless son prodigally squandering away that substance which his father had, with anxious solicitude, been his whole life amassing. We have him at the age of nineteen or twenty, raw from the University of Oxford, just arrived at home, upon the death of his father. Eager to know the possessions he is master of, the old wardrobes are wrenched open, the strong chests unlocked, the parchments tumbled out, and the bags of gold which had long been hoarded up with griping care, are now exposed to the pilfering hands of those about him.

Hogarth pinx.   T. Cook sculp.

RAKE'S PROGRESS.

PLATE II.

" *Prosperity* (with harlot's smiles,
" Most pleasing when she most beguiles),
" How soon, sweet foe, can all thy train
" Of false, gay, frantic, loud, and vain,
" Enter the unprovided mind,
" And memory in fetters bind?
" Load faith and love with golden chain,
" And sprinkle *Lethe* o'er the brain !
" *Pleasure*, on her silver throne,
" Smiling comes, nor comes alone;
" *Venus* comes with her along,
" And smooth *Lyæus*, ever young ;
" And in their train, to fill the press,
" Come *apish Dance*, and *swoln Excess*,
" Mechanic *Honour*, vicious *Taste*,
" And *Fashion* in her changing vest."

HOADLEY.

WE are next to consider him as launched into the world. Having equipped himself with all the necessaries to constitute him a man of taste, he plunges at once into all the fashionable excesses, and enters with spirit into the character he assumes.

The avarice of the penurious father then is contrasted, in this print, with the giddy profusion of his prodigal son. We view him here at his levee, attended by masters of various professions, offering their services. The foremost figure is readily known to be a dancing master ; behind him are two men, noted for teaching the art of defence by different weapons, and who are here drawn from the life; one of whom is a Frenchman, teacher of the small sword, making a thrust with his foil; the other an Englishman, master of the quarter-staff ; the vivacity of the first, and the cold contempt visible in the face of the second, beautifully describe the natural disposition of the two nations. On the left of the latter stands an improver of gardens, drawn also from the life, offering a plan for that purpose. In the chair sits a professor of music, at the harpsichord, running over the keys, waiting to give his pupil a lesson.

Hogarth pinx.   T. Cook sculp.

RAKE'S PROGRESS.

PLATE III.

" O vanity of youthful blood,
" So by misuse to poison good!
" Woman, fram'd for social love,
" Fairest gift of powers above,
" Source of every household blessing;
" All charms in innocence possessing :
" But, turn'd to vice, all plagues above ;
" Foe to thy being, foe to love!
" Guest divine, to outward viewing;
" Ablest minister of ruin !
" And thou, no less of gift divine,
" Sweet poison of misus'd wine !
" With freedom led to ev'ry part,
" And secret chamber of the heart,
" Dost thou thy friendly host betray
" And shew thy riotous gang the way
" To enter in, with covert treason,
" O'erthrow the drowsy guard of reason,
" To ransack the abandon'd place,
" And revel there with wild excess?"

THIS plate exhibits our licentious prodigal engaged in one of his midnight festivities, revelling at a tavern, supposed to be the Rose, in Drury Lane, (a house noted at that time for the reception of abandoned women) with a number of those ragged unfortunate girls, of which the streets of London in an evening are full. Having *beat the rounds*, overset a constable of the night, and knocked down a watchman, evidenced by the staff and broken lanthorn, which he is supposed to have brought off with him in triumph, together with his naked sword, which he was not able to re-sheath, behold this deluded son of dissipation in a sad state of beastial intoxication. In this state he is robbed of his watch, and of every thing of value, by the girl whose hand is in his bosom. In the early part of the evening the company is supposed, from the covering of the floor, and the destruction of the furniture, *viz.* the torn picture and the broken looking-glass, to have been at high romps; tired, however, at last with such wild sort of merriment, they are now seated in order to indulge their loose inclinations, glut their insatiable throats with liquor, and feast their ears.

RAKES PROGRESS

PLATE IV.

" O vanity of youthful blood,
" So by misuse to poison good!
" Reason awakes, and views unbarr'd
" The sacred gates he wish'd to guard;
" Approaching, see the harpy *Law*,
" And *Poverty*, with icy paw,
" Ready to seize the poor remains
" That vice has left of all his gains.
" Cold *penitence*, lame *after-thought*,
" With fear, despair, and horror fraught,
" Call back his guilty pleasures dead,
" Whom he hath wrong'd, and whom betray'd."

BY such excesses as those, which we have witnessed, 'tis no wonder our hero should at last be reduced, for wealth profusely spent wastes as liquor from a leaking cask: as a proof of this, see him stopt in his career by the hand of a sheriff's officer; arrested as he is going to court, it being the birth day of the late Queen, which happened on the first of March, the day sacred to the tutelar saint of Wales. This sufficiently appears by the significant strut of the Welchman, proud of the enormous leek, which in honour of the day, he carries in his hat. During this unexpected disaster of our fashionable spendthrift, the young woman he formerly seduced, and whom Providence had made the mistress of a little money, in the millinery way, very opportunely passes by, and with a heart full of tenderness and affection, gives him a convincing proof of her continued love, returns his baseness with unmerited kindness,—pays the debt and sets him at liberty. Hence we perceive the virtuous constancy of the female sex, whose affection, when once rooted, the severest treatment can hardly alienate; and on the contrary, the fickle disposition and killing cruelty of the other, which prides itself in the ruin of virgin innocence, and glories in acts of studied barbarity. In this view of St. James's, we have at the same time that of *White's*, a house, against which, for its continued iniquity, heaven seems now to direct its severest vengeance. By way of contrast, and to shew us that the true spirit of gaming subsists as well in low life, as in the higher ranks, our author has humourously represented an assembly of shoe-blacks.

RAKES PROGRESS.

PLATE V.

" New to the school of hard *mishap*,
" Driven from the ease of fortune's lap,
" What schemes will nature not embrace
" T' avoid less shame of dread distress?
" *Gold* can the charms of youth bestow,
" And mask deformity with shew;
" Gold can avert the sting of shame,
" In Winter's arms create a flame:
" Can couple youth with hoary age,
" And make antipathies engage."

THIS unexpected arrest, which we have witnessed, is only the fore-runner of like misfortunes to our hero, being, as it were, the beginning of his sorrows.   Unable, now, to discharge his just debts, the showers of distress are coming heavy on him; nor has he any other means of sheltering himself from the impending storm, than by an union with an old rich widow, to whom he has made his addresses under the mask of hypocrisy.

Behold him then, in this plate, at the altar, embracing the happy opportunity of recruiting his wasted fortune, by a marriage with this deformed and withered sybil, ordinary even to a proverb, and possessed but of one eye; youth and beauty, though they were the least of his aim, were the reigning object of hers.   Amazing folly of the sex, who pay no regard either to decency or discretion, so they indulge their vanity and satisfy their inclinations!—With respect to the men, money is their only idol; domestic happiness being least regarded, (though we cannot but observe his inward inclinations, by his amorous leer upon the girl behind, even in the most solemn part of the matrimonial service, which his affected bride imagines to be directed to herself, and which she returns with a squint of satisfaction.)   As this wedding was designed to be a private one, they are supposed to have retired for that purpose to the church of *St Mary-le-bone;* but secret as he thought to keep it, it did not fail to reach the ears of the unfortunate young woman, whom he had formerly seduced, and who is here represented as entering with her child and mother, in order to forbid the solemnization.

RAKES PROGRESS.

PLATE VI.

" *Gold,* thou bright son of Phœbus, source
" Of universal intercourse ;
" Of weeping Virtue soft redress ;
" And blessing those who live to bless :
" Yet oft behold this sacred trust,
" The tool of avaricious lust ;
" No longer bond of human kind,
" But bane of every virtuous mind.
" What chaos such misuse attends,
" Friendship stoops to prey on friends ;
" Health, that gives a relish to delight,
" Is wasted with the wasting night ;
" Doubt and mistrust is thrown on *Heaven,*
" And all its power to chance is given.
" Sad purchase of repentant tears,
" Of needless quarrels, endless fears,
" Of hopes of moments, pangs of years!
" Sad purchase of a tortur'd mind,
" To an imprison'd body join'd."

FLUSHED now with money, and once more master of a fortune, one would naturally imagine our hero would have endeavoured to avoid those rocks on which he split before, and be careful not reduce himself to the distressing situation he was so lately in ; on the contrary, however, he hurries into his usual extravagance, with this difference only, that before, he never cherished a single thought of gain ; whereas, he now seems to make it his chief study ; in hopes of adding to his wealth, he rashly takes the most effectual step to lessen it.

View him then in pursuit of his favorite scheme, at a gaming-table, at midnight, in company with gamesters, highwaymen, and sharpers ; for at these public tables all sorts of people are admitted, that have money to play with ; behold him, after a run of ill-luck, upon his knees, in a desperate fit of phrenzy, gnashing his teeth, and imprecating divine vengeance on his head.

Hogarth pinx.t T. Cook sculp.t

RAKES PROGRESS.

PLATE VII.

" Happy the man whose constant thought
" (Though in the school of hardship taught,)
" Can send remonstrance back to fetch
" Treasures from life's earliest stretch ;
" Who, self-approving, can review
" Scenes of past virtues, which shine through
" The gloom of age, and cast a ray
" To gild the evening of his day !
  " Not so the guilty wretch confin'd :
" No pleasures meet his conscious mind ;
" No blessings brought from early youth,
" But broken faith, and wrested truth ;
" Talents idle and unus'd,
" And every trust of Heaven abus'd.
  " In seas of sad reflection lost,
" From horrors still to horrors toss'd,
" *Reason* the vessel leaves to steer,
" And gives the helm to mad *Despair*."

BY a very natural transition Mr. Hogarth has passed his hero from a gaming-house into a prison ; the inevitable consequence of extravagance. He is here represented in a most distressing situation, without a coat to his back, without money, without a friend to help him. Beggared by a course of ill-luck, the common attendant on the gamester, having first made away with every valuable he was master of, and having now no other resource left to retrieve his wretched circumstances, he at last, vainly promising himself success, commences author, and attempts, though inadequate to the task, to write a play, which is lying on the table, just returned with an answer from the manager of the theatre, to whom he had offered it, that his piece would by no means do. Struck speechless with this disastrous occurrence, all his hopes vanish, and his most sanguine expectations are changed into dejection of spirit. To heighten his distress, he is approached by his wife, and bitterly upbraided for his perfidy in concealing from her his former connections (with that unhappy girl, who is here present with her child, the innocent off-spring of her amours, fainting at the sight of his misfortunes, being unable to relieve him farther) and plunging her into those difficulties she never shall be able to surmount.

RAKES PROGRESS.

PLATE VIII.

" *Madness!* thou chaos of the brain,
" What art, that pleasure giv'st and pain ?⎫
" Tyranny of fancy's reign !⎬
" Mechanic *fancy!* that can build
" Vast labyrinths and mazes wild,
" With rule disjointed, shapeless measure,
" Fill'd with *horror,* fill'd with *pleasure !*
" Shapes of *horror,* that would even
" Cast doubt of mercy upon Heaven;
" Shapes of *pleasure,* that but seen,
" Would split the shaking sides of *Spleen.*
  " O vanity of age ! here see
" The stamp of Heaven effac'd by thee!
" The headstrong course of youth thus run,
" What comfort from this darling son ?
" His rattling chains with terror hear,
" Behold death grappling with despair !
" See him by thee to ruin sold,
" And curse *thyself,* and curse thy *gold !"*

SEE our hero then in the scene before us, raving in all the dismal horrors of hopeless insanity, in the hospital of Bethlehem, the senate of mankind, where each man may find a representative ; there we behold him trampling on the first great law of nature, tearing himself to pieces with his own hands, and chained by the leg to prevent any further mischief he might either do to himself or others. Madness, sad blemish of our nature ! Still, even in this doleful place, we behold our hero followed by his former mistress ; and are hence shewn the wonderful effects of love and friendship ; which will stand firm and unshaken in the storms of distress, and will not desert us, even amid the soul-distracting tempest of adversity. Our artist, in this scene of horror, has taken an opportunity of pointing out to us the various causes of mental blindness ; for such, surely, it may be called, when the intuitive faculties are either destroyed or impaired. In one of the inner rooms of this gallery, No. 54, is a despairing wretch, imploring Heaven for mercy, whose brain is crazed with lip-labouring superstition, the most dreadful enemy of human kind ; which, attended with ignorance, error, penance and indulgence, too often deprives its unhappy votaries of their senses. The next in view is one man drawing lines upon a wall, in order, if possible, to find out the longitude ; and another, before him, looking through a paper, by way of telescope .

RAKES PROGRESS.

THE HARLOT'S PROGRESS.

PLATE I.

IN this age, when wickedness seeks to entrap the unwary; and man, that artful deceiver, racks his invention for wiles to delude the innocent, and to rob them of their virtue; it is more particularly necessary to warn the rising generation of their impending danger, and to lay before the female world the perils to which it is exposed, by opening to their view a sight of that wretchedness that will inevitably be the consequence of their misconduct; and by a timely admonition, to prevent, if possible, the irrevocable misfortunes attendant on a life of prostitution, brought on, perhaps, in an unguarded moment. This was the design of Hogarth in the History of the Harlot before us, in the prosecution of which he has minutely pictured out the most material scenes of her life, from the time of her fall from virtue, to the hour of her death; a history of such interesting circumstances, as must certainly give the unthinking maid a sense of her danger, and alarm her lest she also become a prey to the wiles of the seducer.

The first scene of this domestic tragedy is laid at the Bull Inn, in Wood-Street, Cheapside: the heroine of the piece, about sixteen years of age, is supposed to be just alighted from the York waggon, on its arrival in the inn yard, accompanied by her father on horseback, in search of better fortune. That this was her father's view, is evident from the recommendation, whose direction he is reading. His extreme necessity is plainly indicated by the appearance both of him and his horse, a sorry, broken-knee'd, and foundered animal, who is eagerly catching at a mouthful of straw, in which some earthen vessels are packed; and so full is his master of the business he is upon, as to pay no attention to the damage it occasions.

HARLOTS PROGRESS.

PLATE II.

ENTERED into the path of infamy, the next scene exhibits our young heroine a mistress living in the midst of splendour and profusion : having quitted her innocence with her modesty of attire, she now keeps up the spirit of the character she professes, in giving way to extravagance and inconstancy ; the first being evident from the monkey's being suffered to drag about her head dress, and the latter from the general tenor of the piece. By the Scripture-pieces that ornament her room, we learn that so seared is the conscience of the sinner, as not to be awakened by any distant admonition ; nay more, they gloss over a foul and corrupt life with the colour of religion. The unexpected visit of her keeper, gives a general alarm, and instantly calls forth the subtile invention both of her and her maid, in order to devise some means of her spark's escape ; but as an intriguing woman is seldom at a loss in this respect, she readily effects that, by quarrelling .

Though this scheme answered her present purpose, yet by the continuance of such practices, she is at last discovered, either through her own indiscretion, or the treachery of her servants ; for the wretches that enter such employ, are no longer true to their trust, than while they are partaking of the extravagance of their mistresses. This fatal discovery of inconstancy puts a new face on things : she is instantly discarded and left to begin the world a-new.

HARLOTS' PROGRESS.

PLATE III.

OBSERVE here the child of misfortune fallen from her high estate. Every valuable she once possessed is now gone ; her silver tea-kettle, converted into a tin pot ; and her splendid toilette, once decorated with costly boxes, changed into an old leaf-table, covered with the filthy equipage of her night's revel, and ornamented with a piece of broken looking-glass ; her magnificent apartment in a reputable neighbourhood, is now dwindled into a beggarly room in the purlieus of Drury, as is plain from the inscription on the pewter pots ; and she that once breakfasted in state, is now doomed to make the best of the sad reverse. There was a time when none but the best and most costly wines could please her ; but she is now obliged to cheer her spirits, or banish reflection, with a miserable regale of gin and beer. Having nothing valuable of her own, she now commences a dishonest career, and sends out a watch to pawn, which, perhaps, she had stolen from her last gallant. Her depravity is further evident from the wig box on the tester of the bed, which we are told by the name outside, formerly belonged to one James Dalton, a notorious street-robber, afterwards hanged; a sufficient proof what kind of company she now keeps. It is not beggary only that is the lot of these unhappy wretches, but disease also lends its baneful influence to heighten their misery, as is intimated by the phials, &c. in the window. The person of our heroine is also in unison with the whole. Her laced head-dress, and the tawdry cloak hanging over the chair, may be considered as necessaries of her profession,—serving to conceal a loathsome body, and to attract the eyes of unwary youth. For though her countenance still exhibits a few traces of that beauty which in the first print attracted our notice, it is bloated and marked with disease; indeed disorder and indecency characterise her throughout.

Mr. Hogarth has here taken an opportunity of shewing us the great degeneracy of the age in matters of religion, by laying on the table a piece of butter wrapt up in the title-page of a Pastoral Letter, which a great prelate about that time addressed to his diocese. Indeed every object in this wretched receptacle, presents a dreary and comfortless appearance.

HARLOTS PROGRESS.

PLATE IV.

WE here then behold our wretched female lodged in company with pick-pockets, sharpers, and others of her own stamp, of all ranks and ages, reduced to the miserable alternative of beating hemp, or receiving the correction of the keeper; exposed to the derision of all around, for even her own servant, who seems well acquainted with the place, cannot refrain from insulting her, though her stockings, which she is tying up, together with her shoes, were presents from her mistress, and ought to have reminded her of the gratitude she owed her.   In this horrid receptacle various kinds of punishment are inflicted, according to the degree of obstinacy in the offenders: some are obliged to drag a heavy clog locked to their legs; some are stapled to the ground; while others are hung for an hour by the wrists, or fastened to a post and whipped; but all are made to labour hard, being subject to the correction of a savage task-master, who reaps the profits of their labour.

To shew that neither the dread nor endurance of the severest punishment will deter from the perpetration of crimes, a one-eyed female, close to the keeper, is picking a pocket.   The torn card may probably be dropped by the well-dressed gamester, who has exchanged the dice-box for the mallet, and whose laced hat is hung up as a companion trophy to the hoop petticoat.

One of the girls appears scarcely in her teens.   To the disgrace of our police, these unfortunate little wanderers are still suffered to take their nocturnal rambles in the most public streets of the metropolis.   What heart so void of sensibility as not to heave a pitying sigh at their deplorable situation? Vice is not confined to colour, for a black woman is ludicrously exhibited as suffering the penalty of those frailties which are imagined peculiar to the fair.

HARLOTS PROGRESS.

PLATE V.

RELEASED from confinement, we now view her expiring in all the extremity of penury and wretchedness. What must have been her thoughts at this awful moment? At this distressful hour, no doubt, her manifold sins stood up as her accusers, and as the vital spark took its flight, she felt she could only, with humble resignation, rely on the infinite mercies of that judge, whose authority she had too long set at nought. The two quacks, whose injudicious treatment had probably accelerated her end, are absolutely quarrelling whose medicine was the best, and over-turn the table, without paying the least attention to their expiring patient. A manifest token of the self-sufficiency of these wretches, who are ever ready to prey upon the credulity of the poor and ignorant. That this inattention to any but ourselves is too general among all ranks of people, is shewn by the nurse's rifling her mistress's trunk for plunder, ere the breath has well left her body, to the total neglect of those necessary and friendly offices we are bound to do for one another; and so occupied are her thoughts on what she is upon, as to be perfectly absent to what passes in the room. The only one properly engaged, is the child, (the innocent fruit of her crimes) busied in turning the meat that is roasting at the fire.

In this pitiable situation, without a friend to close her dying eyes, or soften her sufferings by a tributary tear; forlorn! destitute! and deserted! the heroine of this eventful history expires; her premature death brought on by a licentious life, seven years of which had been devoted to debauchery and dissipation, and attended by consequent infamy, misery, and disease. The whole story affords a valuable lesson to the young and inexperienced, and proves this great, this important truth, that a deviation from virtue, is a departure from happiness.

HARLOTS PROGRESS.

PLATE VI.

THE adventures of our heroine being at an end, it is probable, that in the print before us, our artist designed to convey some important moral; at the same time that he has taken an opportunity of indulging his humour, though at the expence of his consistency; for we may notice that the room presents many things which are never met with at the funerals of the poor; such as the escutcheon, (*viz.* the arms of her profession, three spigots and fossets,) the giving of gloves and mourning rings, &c. This however shews the folly of mankind in making expensive funerals, particularly of those who can ill afford it; but such is the general pride, we are always aiming at something above our sphere; the poor apeing the vanities of the rich. We dress up the dead for public view, as on a bridal day, and take care to adorn our persons with all the outward formalities of grief, as if our future good fortune depended on the elegant appearance we made. That this was the painter's meaning, is evident from one of the women viewing the body, and another tricking herself out before the glass. The company here assembled, are supposed to be of our heroine's profession; and as it has been remarked that none are more saintly than "a w—e at a christening," so it may be here observed that none seem more distressed at a funeral. In the corner sits an old procuress, howling for the dead, with a bottle of nantz by her side. Hence we are taught, in the first place, that these wretches have so long made hypocrisy their trade, as to have tears at will; for so steeled are their hearts to any degree of tenderness, that they cannot be presumed to proceed from sorrow: and in the second, that amidst all their seeming concern, they miss no opportunity of drinking, under a pretence of recruiting their wasting spirits. One would naturally imagine that at this silent scene of mortality, the voice of conscience would be heard; but on the contrary we see the heart obstinately shut to its loudest calls, and a propensity to stifling the first spiritual emotions of reflective thought.—View then the undertaker, unappalled by the ghastly corpse, fixing his lustful eye upon the woman, whose glove he is pulling on, and she unaffected at the awful solemnity, artfully robbing him of his handkerchief.

HARLOTS PROGRESS.

THE TIMES OF THE DAY.

MORNING.

THE just analogy between Painting and Poetry has been matter of long observation; each art equally affecting the passions, through the channel of different senses : indeed, so great is their similarity, that they, in some sort, partake of each other's peculiar properties. In poetry we see with our ears, and in painting we hear with our eyes. Poets have been frequently luxurious in the rural descriptions of the different parts of the day, and by a faithful delineation of nature, have pleased the imagination and delighted the understanding. Our author, in the prosecution of his studies in the sister art, has, in his turn, given us a humourous representation of such scenes as occur at those particular times in the metropolis; which may serve as a burlesque to the other, and will give those who have not an opportunity of being present, some idea of what passes beyond the circle of their own immediate knowledge.

The place from whence this scene is taken is Covent Garden; the time, break of day, or Morning; and the season, Winter, (evident from the icicles and snow upon the tops of the houses ;) yet, cold as it is, we have here an old maid going to seven o'clock prayers, whose half-starved, shivering servant behind her, carrying her prayer-book, presents a fine contrast to his stiff mistress.

MORNING.

PLATE II.

NIGHT.

—

THE last plate in this set is a description of Night, and that a night of rejoicing, *viz.* the 29th of May; evident from the bonfires, the oaken bough upon the barber's pole, and the oak leaves fixed in the freemasons' hats. The scene is taken from the narrow part of Charing Cross, as it formerly stood before the way was widened, looking from Whitehall, and exhibits the Rummer Tavern on one side, and the Cardigan's Head on the other; at that time two noted bagnios. We see here the Salisbury flying coach, just set out from the inn, overturning, and its passengers in the utmost fright, increased by the entrance of a burning serpent into the coach, thrown by some unlucky boy. On the other side a waiter is leading home a freemason in his apron, overpowered with liquor, who, by a cut on his face, is shewn to have been in a fray; he is scarcely out of one dilemma, before he is in another, for a maid, from a window in the Rummer Tavern, is showering her favours upon his head. On the right of this man is the house of a barber surgeon, illuminated with candles, whose sign is a hand drawing a tooth, the head in exquisite pain; beneath is written, " Shaving, bleeding, and teeth drawn with a touch." " *Ecce signum,*" behold the sign. An emblem of the operator's abilities. And through the window we have a view of the joint operation of shaving and bleeding, by a drunken 'prentice. Beneath is a beggar's bagnio, a place to which such poor wretches as cannot find a better lodging, are obliged to resort in common. Though dark, we are able to discern these poor creatures by the light of the boy's link, which he is blowing in order to kindle a squib. Behind is a nightman, employed in his profession; and further back, a family carrying off their goods by stealth, fearing they should fall a prey to their landlord.

NIGHT.

BEER-STREET AND GIN-LANE.

PLATE I.

BEER-STREET.

" Beer, happy product of our isle,
  " Can sinewy strength impart;
" When wearied with fatigue and toil,
  " Can cheer each manly heart.

" Labour and art, upheld by thee,
  " Successfully advance;
" We quaff the balmy juice with glee,
  " And water leave to France.

" Genius of health, thy grateful taste,
  " Rivals the cup of Jove;
" And warms each English, generous breast,
  " With liberty and love."

IN this print our author offers to our view a representation of John Bull in his happiest moments : a general cessation of work, and all parties regaling themselves with a refreshing draught of the cheering liquor, porter. On the left we have a group of jovial tap-house politicians,—a butcher, a drayman, and a cooper. The drayman is deceitfully whispering some soft things to a servant maid, who is all attention to what she hears; and by her having the key of the street-door with her, she is supposed to have stept out of some neighbouring house at dinner time, for a tankard of porter, which the family is waiting for. The butcher is nearly splitting his sides with laughter, to see the girl so easily imposed on.

BEER STREET.

PLATE II.

GIN-LANE.

———

" Gin, cursed fiend! with fury fraught,
  " Makes human race a prey;
" It enters by a deadly draught,
  " And steals our life away.

" Virtue and Truth, driv'n to despair,
  " Its rage compels to fly,
" But cherishes, with hellish care,
  " Theft, murder, perjury.

" Damn'd cup! that on the vitals preys,
  " That liquid fire contains;
" Which madness to the heart conveys,
  " And rolls it thro' the veins."

AS a contrast to the last print, we observe in this, the pernicious effects of British Spirits among the poor. Here the scene of health and gladness is vanished, and that of disease and wretchedness introduced. As we remarked, in Beer Street, the houses to be fair and good-conditioned, excepting that of the pawnbroker's, which was ready to fall, so we perceive the houses here, in general, old and ruinous, excepting that of *Master Gripe's*. By this we are taught that poverty is the usual attendant on gin-drinking, and that where this vice prevails, none are known to thrive, but such as feed upon the property of others. This abominable liquor is, among the vulgar, very justly called by the name of *Strip-me-naked*, it being found to waste the substance of those poor wretches that accustom themselves to the drinking it, by a continual drain, not leaving them at last the bare necessaries of life; for this infatuating poison leads them on, and almost obliges them to repair the gnawings of one dram, by the burning aid of a second.

GIN LANE.

SOUTHWARK FAIR.

———

THE subject of the plate under consideration is that of the Borough Fair; a fair held some time since in the Borough of Southwark, though now suppressed. This fair was attended, generally, by the inhabitants of town and country, and therefore, was one that afforded great variety; especially as before its suppression, it was devoted to every thing loose and irregular. A view of the scene, of which the following print is a faithful representation, will affirm this truth.

The principal view upon the left represents the fall of a scaffold, on which was assembled a strolling company, pointed out, by the paper lanthorn hanging in front, to be that belonging to Cibber and Bullock, ready dressed to exhibit "The Fall of Bajazet." Here we see merry-andrews, monkeys, queens and emperors sinking in one general confusion; and that the crash may appear the greater, the stand beneath is humourously supposed to consist of earthenware and china. Notwithstanding this fatal overthrow, few below are seen to notice it; witness the boys and woman gambling at the box and dice, the upright monkey, and the little bag-piper dancing his wooden figures. Above this scaffold hangs a painting, the subject of which is the *stage mutiny*; whose figures are as follow:—On one side is Pistol, (strutting and crying out " *Pistol's alive*,") Falstaff, Justice Shallow, and many other characters of Shakespear. On the other, the manager bearing in his hand a paper, on which is written, "*it cost £6,000;*" a scene painter who has laid his brushes aside, and taken up a cudgel; and a woman holding an ensign, bearing the words, " *We'll starve 'em out*." In the corner is a man, quiet and snug, hugging a bag of money, laughing at the folly of the rest; and behind, a monkey, perched upon a sign iron, supposed to be that of the Rose Tavern in Drury Lane, squeaking out " *I am a gentleman*."

SOUTHWARK FAIR.

THE COMPANY OF STROLLERS.

IF variety is any ways entertaining, or if the life of a painting consists in its diversity of figures, the piece before us claims our particular attention; none does more abound with contrasted subjects, nor can the *vis comica* be more conspicuous: every group is crowded with humour, every subject with matter of laughter. Here we see confusion mixed with uniformity, and inconsistency united with propriety; royalty let down by the ensigns of beggary, and beggary set off by the regalia of royalty. Most people are, indeed, acquainted with stage exhibitions, but few have any idea of their apparatus. Mr. Hogarth, therefore, desirous of communicating that pleasure he frequently enjoyed himself, and of profiting by the design, published this plate in the year 1738, when the attention of the public was called to this class of people, it being just before the act against strolling players took place. Altho' this salutary law put a stop for a time to scenes of this sort, yet new companies, phœnix-like, rose with vigour from the dying embers of former ones; and such companies continue to the present day.

The place from whence this scene is taken is supposed to be a barn, belonging to an inn in some country town, intimated by the corn and flail aloft, the hen and chickens at roost (though here) upon a wave, and the eggs upon the bed. The time is evening, the company from the theatres at London, dressing, and preparing to perform a farce, which, we are told by the play-bill on the bed, is called *The Devil to pay in Heaven*, (a very suitable subject) with entertainments of tumbling and rope dancing. Such, we are to conceive, is their poverty, that they have but one room for all purposes; witness the bed, the gridiron, the urinal, the food, and all the stage apparatus; *viz.* scenes, flags, paint-pots, pageants, brushes, clouds, waves, ropes, besoms, drums, trumpets, salt-boxes, and other musical instruments, crowns, mitres, helmets, targets, dark-lanthorns, cushions, perriwigs, feathers, hampers of jewels, and contrivances for conjuring, thunder, lightning.

STROLLING PLAYERS.

THE ENRAGED MUSICIAN.

AMIDST all the follies of the age, there never was a greater than the immoderate passion of the people for music. Though amusement and recreation are sometimes necessary, yet when carried to excess, they become vitious. Now, so far did the luxury of this kingdom extend at the time when this plate was first published, which was in the year 1741, that Italians (as being supposed to be the greater proficients) were brought over at considerable expence; and the poorest and least skilled among them, who from a want of ability, or a want of means, could not continue in their own country, soon discovering our folly, gathered here in flocks and took possession of the place. When here, they were encouraged, and their wretched abilities looked upon as supernatural; they introduced a new stile of music, which suited well the growing levity of this nation. The noble and elevated was immediately transformed into the trifling and insignificant: and the solemn and majestic sounds of British harmony gave place to the tinkling frippery of Italian sing-song.

To ridicule this immoderate passion of the age for music, Mr. Hogarth published this print; in it he represents an Italian professor of music, at his study, enraged to the greatest degree, at the astounding noise the motley group collected beneath the window are making, which seem assembled in order to annoy and distress him. By the inscription on the house over the way, he is also supposed to live in the neighbourhood of a pewterer, whose constant hammering is no trifling annoyance to him. Our artist seems in this plate to have let none of the material or customary noises of London streets escape him. In front are some children at their sports, one of whom is hallooing and beating of a drum; another dragging a tile upon the stones, while a third is winding a racket. On the right is a ballad-singer, bawling out " The Lady's Fall," with a squalling infant in her arms; on the left, a man grinding a cleaver, whose machine is standing on the foot of a dog, and sets him yelping.

Hogarth pinx.   I. Cook sculp.

THE ENRAGED MUSICIAN.

THE SLEEPING CONGREGATION.

IN this sleeping congregation we have a striking instance of the effects of modern oratory. The scene is taken from a country church, the congregation consisting chiefly of the lower class of people, and the ill-judging minister supposed to be addressing them in language they cannot comprehend, which we are to imagine not his own, his vacant face declaring an empty head, and the rising pimples, that he spends more of his time over the bottle than his study. With great humour he is represented as preaching on *Matthew, Chap.* ix. *Verse* 28. " *Come unto me, all ye that labour, and are heavy laden, and I will give you rest ;*" he having, in an eminent degree, the happy talent of quieting a restless body by slumber. The piece before us shews how inattentive the generality of mankind are to matters of the greatest importance ; and from the prayer book (dropping from the hand of the dozing woman) being open at the matrimonial service, we are taught how readily they forego improvement, and prevent serious reflection, by amusing themselves with what they think entertaining. With great propriety is that text of scripture written against the pulpit, " *I am* " *afraid of you, lest I have bestowed upon you labour in vain.*" *Galatians, Chap.* iv. *Verse* 11. The hum-drum drawling manner of the indolent preacher is evident from its effects upon his hearers. Instead of being full of his subject, possessed with the spirit of it, and labouring under the weight of those conceptions which it inspires ; instead of pressing upon the audience with a torrent of tender and manly eloquence, so as to animate the cold, rouse the lethargic, and bend the stubborn ; we see him seated in his pulpit, poring over a discourse, which he delivers in so yawning a tone, that one would suppose him talking in his sleep : nay, by his handkerchief beside him, in continual use, we see that coughing, hawking, and spitting, the defects of other men's rhetoric, are the flowers, the figures, and ornaments of his.

Hogarth pinxt.   T. Cook sculpt.

THE SLEEPING CONGREGATION.

Published by Longman, Hurst, Rees, & Orme, Jan.y 1.st 1809.

PIT TICKET.

———

AS there are few scenes in life, expressing the folly of mankind, that Mr. Hogarth has not taken an opportunity of exposing, so this, among the rest, is worthy of our notice, being, like that of horse racing, one of the fashionable diversions, calculated to support that spirit of gaming, for which this country is distinguished. Exclusive of this, we are persuaded it can afford very little entertainment, unless we delight in cruelty, and find pleasure in giving pain.

Take notice then of this group of gamblers, of all ranks, as well noblemen, as butchers, chimney sweepers, shoe blacks, post boys, thieves, and blackguards of all denominations; we say, noblemen, for to what meanness will not men submit to gratify their reigning passion? Read in their faces the disposition of their hearts. Observe him in the middle, see him lost in the enjoyment of his favourite amusement; eager to bet, and full of cash, he is the ready dupe of every one who pleases to take advantage of his weakness. In this confused state of mind, one villain is purloining a bank note from him; behind him is another, wishing to do the same, and grudging his neighbour the happy opportunity. The next but one above the last noticed, is a blind man, who, with that old sporter on the other side, (supposed to have lost his hearing, and the use of his limbs by age,) is introduced by way of intimation, that so bigotted are we to our particular inclinations, that although we have not powers to indulge them, still are we desirous to partake of the enjoyment, though it be even but a taste. Next the pit, on the left of this plate, is one man registering the bets; another with a bag containing a favourite cock, for a by battle; and near him another, with the utmost eagerness bawling.out " *Ginger* against *Pye*, " for that piece, who says done?" Above, without the pit, is a Frenchman, turning up his nose at this insipid entertainment, and dropping his snuff in the eyes of the man below him.

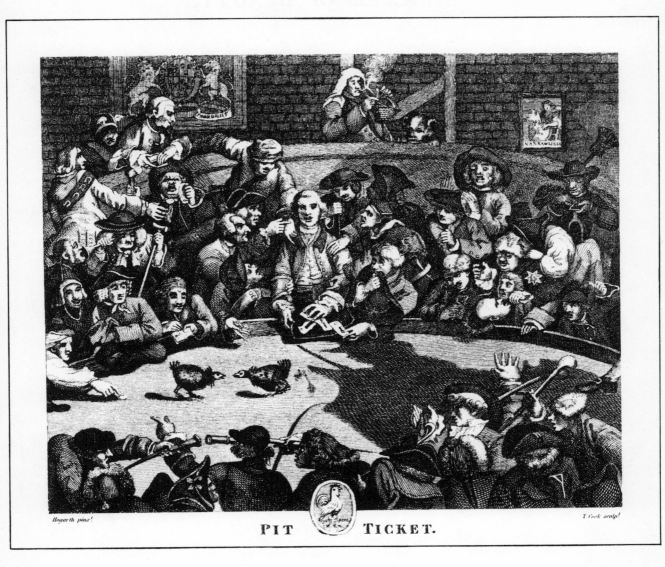

Hogarth pinx!.   T Cook sculp!.

PIT TICKET.

ANALYSIS OF BEAUTY.

———

OUR artist, in his own portrait, engraved as a frontispiece to his works, in 1745, having drawn a serpentine line on a painter's palette, and denominated it *the line of beauty*, found himself frequently involved in disputes, and called upon to explain the qualities of this line; he therefore determined to commence author, and in 1753 published a treatise, entitled the *Analysis of Beauty*, in order to shew that the line of beauty is serpentine, as well as to fix the fluctuating ideas of *taste*, by establishing a standard of beauty.

ANALYSIS OF BEAUTY.

Hogarth pinx?

T. Cook sculp?

THE BEGGAR'S OPERA.

THE title over this print was in capitals, disproportionably large.

> " *Brittons,* attend—view this harmonious stage,
> And listen to those notes which charm the age.
> Thus shall your tastes in *sounds* and *sense* be shown,
> And " Beggar's Op'ras" ever be your own."

No painter or engraver's name. The plate seems at once to represent the exhibition of the " The Beggar's Opera," and the rehearsal of an Italian one.

In the former, all the characters are drawn with the heads of different animals; as Polly with a cat's; Lucy, with a sow's; Macheath, with an ass's; Lockit, and Mr. and Mrs. Peachum, with those of an ox, a dog, and an owl.

In the latter several noblemen appear conducting the chief female singer forward on the stage, and perhaps are offering her money, or protection from a figure that is rushing towards her with a drawn sword. Harmony, flying in the air, turns her back on the English playhouse, and hastens towards the Rival Theatre. Musicians stand in front of the former, playing on the Jew's-harp, the salt-box, the bladder and string, bagpipes, &c. On one side are people of distinction, some of whom kneel as if making an offer to Polly, or paying their adorations to her. To these are opposed a butcher, &c. expressing similar applause. Apollo and one of the Muses are fast asleep beneath the stage. A man is easing nature under a wall hung with ballads, and shewing his contempt of such compositions by the use he makes of one of them. A sign of the star, a gibbet, and some other circumstances less intelligible appear in the back ground.

et cantare pares et responder parati

Harmony

Hogarth pin.ᵗ   L. Cook & Son sc.

THE BEGGARS OPERA.

INHABITANTS OF THE MOON.

ABOUT the year 1750, (if we may judge by the wigs and style of dress) appeared the original of this severe satire on royalty, episcopacy, and law.

The scene is supposed to be in the clouds, where, on a platform, the principal characters are seated. The head of the monarch is either a crown-piece or a guinea. The collar of Esses is ludicrously changed to a string of bubbles; his breast is decorated with a pointed star; and on the top of the globe and sceptre is a crescent, alluding to his lunar situation. Beneath his throne is a circle, perhaps intended as an emblem of perpetuity.

The satire on episcopacy is still more strongly pointed: the face of the bishop is formed of a Jew's harp, which may probably allude to his religious tenets, having arisen out of the doctrines of Judaism. He is pulling a bell rope, that is fastened to the bible, which serves as a lever, to act upon a machine, the lower part of which is a mill, but the upper part a steeple, having a vane at the top of it; and a bell, plainly seen in the act of ringing or working: intimating, that by this instrument he works out of the church those good things, without which he would set little value upon his spiritualities: this treasure falls into a coffer, sarcastically marked as his own, by the armorial bearings, a knife and fork, with the mitre added as a crest. Beneath the episcopal robe peeps a cloven foot; and if we may judge by the weather cock, the motion of the pump is in some degree acted upon by the king, in whose quarter the wind seems to set.

The head of law appears to be made of a large mallet or wedge. To this metaphor we can give no explanation: nor is the enormous size of the sword, which seems to betray more than common justice, an allusion so clearly understood as some other parts of the design.

Some of the Principal Inhabitants of yᵉ MOON, as they Were Perfectly Discover'd by a Telescope brought to yᵉ Greatest Perfection since yᵉ last Eclipse; Exactly Engraved from the Objects, whereby yᵉ Curious may Guess at their Religion, Manners, &c.